Discard

jBIO
WOODS

Collins, David R.

Tiger Woods, golf superstar

CHILDREN: BIOGRAPHY

TIGER WOODS
Golf Superstar

TIGER WOODS
Golf Superstar

By David R. Collins
Illustrated by Larry Nolte

PELICAN PUBLISHING COMPANY
Gretna 1999

To Joey, Scott (T-Bone), Kenny, Jon, Carl, and all the other "Tigers" I have known

Library of Congress Cataloging-in-Publication Data

Collins, David R.
    Tiger Woods / David R. Collins ; illustrated by Larry Nolte.
        p.   cm.
    Summary: A biography of the talented young golfer who won his
first U.S. Amateur Championship in 1994 at age 19 and the Masters
Tournament in Augusta, Georgia, in 1997.
    ISBN 1-56554-321-1 (hardcover : alk. paper)
    1. Woods, Tiger—Juvenile literature. 2. Golfers—United States-
-Biography—Juvenile literature. 3. Racially mixed people—United
States—Biography—Juvenile literature. [1. Woods, Tiger.
2. Golfers. 3. Racially mixed people—Biography.] I. Nolte,
Larry, ill. II. Title.
GV964.W66C65 1998
796.352'092
[B]—DC21   97-30574
                                                    CIP
                                                    AC

Printed in Hong Kong

Published by Pelican Publishing Company, Inc.
1000 Burmaster Street, Gretna, Louisiana 70053

TIGER WOODS, GOLF SUPERSTAR

Tiger Woods is a smiler. People say he smiled from the moment he was born. That was on December 30, 1975, in Cypress, California.

Tiger's real name was Eldrick. His father, Earl Woods, nick-named his son Tiger after a friend he fought with in Vietnam. Eldrick legally changed his name to Tiger in December of 1996.

Baby Tiger liked sitting in his high chair. His father carried the high chair into the garage. Earl Woods hit golf balls into a net. Tiger watched his father and smiled.

Young Tiger liked sitting with his mother too. Kutilda Woods was from a faraway country named Thailand. She read to Tiger and taught him to add and subtract. The boy listened to his mother and smiled.

Tiger's father loved golf. Earl Woods did not get to play when he was a boy. Many thought golf was a sport for white people. He learned to play golf when he was older.

Earl Woods hoped his son would love golf too. The man shortened a golf club just for young Tiger. The boy learned to swing it before he was one year old.

Soon Earl took his son to play on a golf course. Other golfers were amazed. Tiger was the only golfer in diapers. One time his diaper fell down when he hit the ball! Tiger just kept playing.

Earl and Kutilda were proud of their son. They called a TV station when Tiger was two. The television people filmed Tiger playing golf. Everyone was surprised at how good he was!

The next year Tiger played against a famous movie star on TV. His name was Bob Hope. Mr. Hope had played golf for sixty years but Tiger beat him! "He's going to be a pro golfer!" Earl Woods bragged.

Young Tiger loved to play golf with his father. Each day the boy called him at work. "Can we play today?" Tiger asked.

"Sure we can," Earl Woods answered.

Someone checked the rules at the golf course. One rule said no one under the age of ten could play. "That's okay," Earl told Tiger. "We will play somewhere else." That's just what they did!

The golf pro at the new course was amazed. Tiger stood only three feet seven inches tall and weighed fifty pounds. But the boy swung a golf club better than most grown men. "I want to coach you," said Rudy Duran, the golf pro.

When he was five, Tiger appeared on the TV show "That's In-credible." Someone asked for his autograph. Tiger did not know how to write script yet. So he *printed* his name.

Tiger quickly learned how to keep score in golf. In this sport, players try to get the *lowest* score they can. The golfer who hits his or her ball into all the holes with the fewest shots is the winner.

In September of 1981 Tiger started kindergarten. Most of the other students at his school were white. A few of them did not like blacks.

Four sixth graders grabbed Tiger when he arrived at school the first day. They tied him to a tree and called him names. They threw rocks at him. Why? the boy wondered. The older boys were punished, but Tiger never forgot that sad day.

Tiger liked school. His mother's help gave him a head start on other kids in his class. His kindergarten teacher was impressed with how much he knew. She said he could move into first grade right away.

Earl and Kutilda talked the move over. They chose to let Tiger make the decision. He decided to stay with his friends in kindergarten. He was already playing against older boys in golf. He liked being with his own age group in school.

Tiger got his first set of special golf clubs when he was six. They were small so Tiger could handle them. "You won't need a one iron for a while," his coach said. "You can't handle it yet." A one-iron club is a very tall and heavy kind of golf club.

Tiger found his father's one-iron club. It came up to Tiger's chin. Still, he could hit the ball just fine with it. His parents got Tiger his own one-iron club.

Tiger began entering tournaments. His mother drove him to each one. She stayed out of sight while he played. She cheered him up when he lost. "You can't win every time," she told him.
"I know," he answered. "But I sure wish I could."

Sometimes Earl Woods broke the golf-course rules. He yelled when Tiger got ready to hit. He rolled golf balls all over the green. He sang and danced around. "Hey, Tiger, let me hear you growl," his father teased.

At first Tiger *did* growl. "Stop it!" he said. He was angry. But then he understood. His father was teaching Tiger to focus on his golf game. He had to ignore everything else. Now Tiger smiled at his father. The boy's game got better and better.

In 1983, Tiger won his first golf tournament. It was the Optimist International World Tournament. He was eight years old. "He was probably just lucky," someone said. So Tiger won the tournament the next year too!

That was just the first of many tournament wins. He won tournaments around his home. Others were farther away. No young golfer won as many tournaments as Tiger. Trophies started filling up his house. "You might have to sleep outside, Tiger!" Earl Woods laughed.

Most people cheered Tiger. "He's fantastic!" people declared. But there were still those who did not like blacks. Some even made threats against his life. Tiger ignored the threats. He kept playing—and winning. He won the U.S. Junior Amateur Tournament in 1991, 1992, and 1993.

Tiger showed he could win in the classroom too. It was not always easy juggling his school and golf schedule. But Tiger did it.

Earl and Kutilda were proud of the grades their son earned. He was an honors student at Western High School in Anaheim, California. Tiger graduated in 1994.

Tiger knew where he wanted to attend college. When he was thirteen, he had written to the golf coach at Stanford University. Tiger wanted to study accounting at the school. The golf coach wrote back—come ahead! Tiger went to Stanford in 1994 on a full scholarship.

Tiger worked hard on his studies. Yet he also liked to have fun. Sometimes he went dancing. His friends laughed as they watched him. "You may be smooth on a golf course," one buddy said. "But you dance like an octopus." Tiger just smiled.

In 1996 Tiger finished his second year at Stanford. It was difficult studying and playing golf too. He had won the U.S. Amateur Tournament in 1994, 1995, and 1996. Many people urged Tiger to play professional golf. "You can finish your college education later," they said.

As usual, Tiger talked to his parents. As usual, they told Tiger it was *his* decision to make. Tiger decided to leave college and turn pro. "But I know I will finish college," he stated. "Right now I just want to think about golf."

Tiger thinks out everything on the golf course. He grips every club carefully. He judges the way the wind will affect his ball in the air. He knows how his ball will roll when he putts, which means hitting a short shot. He never lets anyone or anything distract him. "You have to stay focused *all* the time," he says.

It's that kind of focus that Tiger took to the Las Vegas Invitational in October, where he won his first professional tournament. That focus got him named "Sportsman of the Year" by *Sports Illustrated,* and then it took him to the Masters Tournament in April of 1997. Many consider the Masters golf's biggest event. It is always held in Augusta, Georgia. Again, there were people there who did not like blacks playing in the tournament. By now, Tiger did not care about those people. If they judged him because of his skin color, that was *their* problem.

The Masters Tournament attracted the best golfers in the world. At twenty-one, Tiger was the youngest. The average age of other golfers was thirty-eight. He was also the only black. One thing was certain—Tiger came to play golf. "I always play to win," he said.

Tiger shot a 70 for eighteen holes of golf on the opening day. Only three golfers beat him. A 70 was considered a fine score. But Tiger did not smile. He knew he could do better.

The next day Tiger shot a 66. That was more like it, he thought. His total for two days of golfing was 136. The golfer in second place was 3 strokes behind, with 139.

On Saturday, Tiger knocked a stroke off his game with a 65. Every shot seemed to go in. His long shots were perfect. His score of 201 was 9 strokes ahead of the golfer in second place. He hoped he could keep up the pace. *Everyone* was watching Tiger Woods.

On the final day of the Masters Tournament, Tiger shot a 69. The four scores added up to 270, 12 strokes ahead of the second-place golfer. Tiger broke the Masters record of 271, set by Jack Nicklaus in 1965. "Tiger is a lot better than I ever was," says Nicklaus. "His shots are so long, he reduces the course to nothing."

A smiling Tiger Woods hugged his father and mother when he won the Masters. President Clinton saw the picture in the newspaper of Tiger hugging his father. The president called Tiger and said that picture was Tiger's "best shot of the day."

No one knows how much money Tiger will earn playing golf. It could be $60,000,000 or more a year! Equipment companies and advertisers know Tiger is a good salesman. They pay him for endorsing their products.

No one knows how many tournaments Tiger could win in his lifetime either. Once people laughed when Jack Nicklaus said Tiger could win the Masters Tournament twenty times. Now, some people think that was a low guess.

Tiger wants kids everywhere to play golf. He helps children in poor neighborhoods get a chance to learn. He helps set up clinics and comes in to teach.

"Golf is a great sport," says Tiger. "And it doesn't matter what color or nationality you are to play it. I'm Cablinasian. I'm part Caucasian, part black, part Indian, and part Asian."

Yes, Tiger Woods has many parts. But when you put them all together, you get a total champion, a superstar, with a winning smile!